Love Yourself

Mrs. J.B. Livingston

Published by

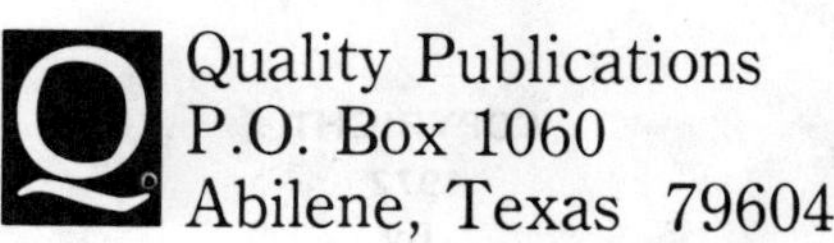

Quality Publications
P.O. Box 1060
Abilene, Texas 79604

ACKNOWLEDGEMENTS

It is impossible to properly acknowledge the source of all the thoughts and ideas that have been contributed by others to this writer. Teachers, preachers, faithful elders, friends, my own beloved mother all made their contributions. Church bulletins, newsletters, religious periodicals have made their contributions. Those widely known "fellows", Selected, Copied, and Anonymous, have made their contributions. My sincere thanks to all who have made this work possible.

Above all, I thank my Lord and Savior Jesus Christ for His word whereby we have the faith to desire a better way of life; and I thank my wonderful husband who taught me to love myself!

FOREWORD

This is a Bible-oriented work. The author believes there is an Omnipotent God and that the Bible is the inspired Word of that God. She also believes that God created man in His image and that in Him we live, move, and have our existence. She believes He is the supreme authority for man's way of life on the earth He created, and that obedience to His law is the only way to have Life with Him after the grave. She believes that when the new heavens and the new earth come into existence that only those who have loved and obeyed God will find their names written in the Book of Life and that those whose names are not found in the Book of Life will be cast into the lake of fire, which is the second death.

The author also believes that to live the Christian life is the only way to find peace in this life - that those whose God is the Lord are the happiest people on His earth.

If you are one of the many who believe that the Bible is only a myth or a fable you will not appreciate nor enjoy reading the book. Please have the courtesy and respect to withhold any critique on it until you have carefully read it; if you do not read it you are not qualified to make a critique on it. It is dishonest to judge anything until we have informed ourselves on that thing to the very best of our ability.

"Now to Him who is able by the power at work in us to do far more abundantly than all that we ask or think, to Him be glory in the church and in Christ Jesus to all generations, for ever and ever. Amen." (Ephesians 3:20, 21.)

Mrs. J. B. Livingston

INTRODUCTION

In Leviticus 19:18, and again in verse 34, the statement is found "thou shalt love thy neighbor as thyself". Seven times in the New Testament this statement is quoted; four times it is recorded as being quoted by Jesus - Matthew 19:19; 22:39; Mark 12:31 and Luke 10:25-37; twice it is quoted by Paul, Romans 13:9, and Galatians 5:14; and by James in James 2:8. James says, "If you really fulfill the royal law, according to the scripture, 'you shall love your neighbor as yourself' you do well."

For many years this statement provoked many questions. These questions were put to teachers, preachers, elders, and others who commanded respect because of their Bible knowledge, but no satisfactory answer was given.

"Love thy neighbor as thyself" indicates that one is to love self, yet there is constantly presented the caution that one is not to overrate himself. Is the statement actually paradoxical?

While preparing lesson material on the book of Leviticus the discovery was made that God gave many specific commands to His people regarding their relationship with their neighbor. A detailed study of some of these teachings began to provide the long-sought-for answers to some of the questions regarding one's love for self.

Diligent and prayerful study has resulted in the development of twelve facets of "love . . . . yourself". May a sharing of the things found in this study make a contribution to the reader in increasing his love for himself.

Mrs. J. B. Livingston

TABLE OF CONTENTS

Chapter 1

LOVE . . . YOURSELF

It seems that by nature we are a negative people. In the very beginning God told the man that the day he ate of the tree of knowledge of good and evil he would die. Satan came along and said, "You will not die", and man yielded to the temptation to partake of the forbidden fruit.

One of our most used words is *don't.* It is the word our children hear most often, *don't* do, *don't* go, *don't* say. It is the word we use in our own self-defense; I *don't* do this, I *don't* do that; I must be a pretty fine fellow for I *don't* do anything much.

In God's law we look for the "shall nots", and often try to justify our actions by saying there is no "shall not" to forbid what we have done.

A positive approach is needed, yet the negative has its place. In our study of "Love . . . . Yourself" we shall, of necessity, use the positive and the negative. God told Israel *you shall not hate* your brother but *you shall love* your neighbor as yourself.

James in James 2:8 says the royal law according to the scripture is "you shall love your neighbor as yourself".

How am I to love my neighbor? As I love myself! The very statement indicates that to love myself is a requirement in fulfilling God's royal law.

Perhaps much of the trouble in our world hinges on the fact that we do not know *how* to love ourselves, hence, we do not know *how* to love our neighbor.

The logical place to start this study is with the meaning of the word love which can be applied to our topic, love yourself. Let us consider three sources: 1. Webster's dictionary definition, 2. Paul's discourse listing the characteristics of love in I Corinthians 13:4-8, and 3. God's instructions pertaining to loving one's neighbor.

1. Webster's dictionary definition

(n) a. a feeling of strong personal attachment induced by sympathetic understanding, or by ties of kinship; ardent affection.

b. the benevolence attributed to God as being like a father's affection for his children.

c. a strong liking, fondness, good will.

(v.t.) a. to have or manifest love for

b. to take delight or pleasure in

2. I Corinthians 13:4-8 J. B. Phillips translation (with RSV in parenthesis)

This love of which I speak is slow to lose patience, it looks for a way of being constructive (patient and kind). It is not possessive (jealous), it is neither anxious to impress (boastful) nor does it cherish inflated ideas of its own importance (not arrogant). Love has good manners (not rude) and does not pursue selfish advantage (does not insist on its own way). It is not touchy (not irritable). It does not keep account of evil (not resentful) or gloat over the wickedness of other people (does not rejoice in wrong). On the contrary, it is glad with all good men when truth prevails (rejoices in the right (truth, KJV)). Love knows no limit to its endurance (bears all things), no end to its trust (believes all things), no fading of its hope (hopes all things); it can outlast anything (endures all things). It is, in fact, the one thing that still stands when all else has fallen (love never ends).

Henry Drummond in his classic THE GREATEST THING IN THE WORLD gives the following characteristics as ingredients of love: patience, kindness, generosity, humility, courtesy, unselfishness, good temper, guilelessness and sincerity. To read this treatise would be good homework in connection with this study.

3. God's instruction pertaining to relationship with one's neighbor.

Leviticus 19:16-18. You shall not go up and down as a slanderer among your people, and you shall not stand forth against the life of your neighbor. I am the Lord. You shall not hate your brother in your heart, but you shall reason with your neighbor, lest you bear sin because of him. You shall not take vengeance or bear any grudge against the sons of your own people, but you shall love your neighbor as yourself: I am the Lord.

In this reading we find God using *people, your neighbor, your brother,* and *the sons of your people* interchangeably. This broadens our scope of study, for often we separate our neighbors from our brothers and our people, and sometimes show more love and courtesy to those we call neighbors than we show our brothers and our families.

Romans 13:10. Love does no wrong to a neighbor. Phillips reads, love hurts none.

Exodus 20:16. You shall not bear false witness against your neighbor.

Ephesians 4:25. Let everyone speak the truth with his neighbor.

These three sources give us a foundation upon which to build and develop twelve facets of loving ourselves.

"Love . . . . Yourself."

Discussion Questions

1. *Quote from memory James 2:8.*
2. *How is one to love one's neighbor?*
3. *In your own thoughts state what it means to love yourself.*
4. *Do you love yourself?*
5. *In what way do you love or not love yourself?*
6. *Give at least three facets of Webster's definition of love.*
7. *Which, if any, describes your love for yourself?*
8. *What are the characteristics of love as stated by Paul in 1 Corinthians 13:4-8?*
9. *From your concordance list the instructions God gives His people pertaining to their relationships with their neighbors.*
10. *Do you love your neighbor as yourself?*

Chapter 2

UNDERSTAND YOURSELF

It has been said, "Understanding ourselves is essential to understanding others". The primary facet of loving self used in this study will be understanding self. Webster defines love as a feeling of strong personal attachment induced by sympathetic understanding.

To understand ourselves it is needful to start at the beginning. In Genesis 2 we find recorded the generations of the heaven and the earth when they were created. In verse 7, we read that the Lord God formed man of dust from the ground and breathed into his nostrils the breath of life, and man became a living soul. From the very beginning we see man as a dual being, the *earth* man and the *spirit* man.

After the woman and the man had sinned God told the man he would live by the sweat of his face till he returned to the ground from which he was taken, *for dust thou art, and unto dust shalt thou return* (Genesis 3:19).

In Ecclesiastes 12:7 Solomon said, "the dust returns to the earth as it was: and the spirit returns to God who gave it." Paul, in his treatise on the resurrection in I Corinthians 15:42-46 discusses the physical body and the spiritual body. James in 2:26, says the body without the spirit is dead.

Men throughout the ages have recognized the dual make-up of man, even our poets. Henry Wadsworth Longfellow in his classic poem, A PSALM OF LIFE, wrote:

Life is real, life is earnest,
And the grave is not its goal.
Dust thou art, to dust returneth,
Was not spoken of the soul.

Yet, with this recognition, few people seem to understand this dual being.

Paul wrote the Corinthians that the body, or earth man, was made to house the spirit which God gave it. (I Corinthians 3:16; 6:13-20.) There is an eternal conflict between the two, because the earth man desires to serve the lust of the flesh, the lust of the eye and the pride of life, while the spirit man desires to love and obey God.

Paul expresses his inner battle in Romans 7:15-25, when he says he does not understand his own actions, for the good he wants to do he does not do, and the wrong he does not want to do he does; that when he wants to do good evil is always present, so he pommeled or buffeted his body to bring it into subjection to the spirit. In Romans 8:4-6 Paul states that those who live according to the flesh have their minds on the flesh, and those who have their minds on the spirit live according to the spirit.

To set the mind on the flesh is death, and
To set the mind on the spirit is life and peace.

Now what do we have? The earth man whose function is to house the spirit man, and a constant battle for domination.

To set the mind on the flesh, and make the spirit serve the flesh is DEATH!	 E | S	Death
To set the mind on the spirit, and make the flesh serve the spirit is LIFE AND PEACE!	 E | S	Life and Peace

The solution to the battle is found in Romans 8:13, we put to death the deeds of the body by the spirit.

After this life the flesh goes back to the dust and the soul returns to God. If this is true, then, what is the hang-up? This is not "all there is". The story of man does not end there. Romans 14:12, "So each of us shall give account of himself to God." Jesus, in John 5:28,29, says all will come forth, those who have done good to the resurrection of life and those who have done evil to the resurrection of judgment. John was told to write in Revelation 20:13 that all will be judged by what they have done; and those who have served the flesh man will be cast into the lake of fire. This is the second death.

Our present day Playboy philosophy of free-love, premarital sex activity, the relativity of good and evil, is animalistic, and has degraded woman to the very depths - she is no more than common chattel to be bought, sold, and used for the animal desires of man.

Today we hear much about *fulfillment*; everyone is seeking *fulfillment*. We read much and hear more about the lack of *fulfillment*. Dear Reader, there is *NO FULFILLMENT IN A LIFE WHICH LEAVES OUT GOD*. We must understand that we were created a dual being with an innate desire and need for God in our lives.

SELF-DISCOVERY

Within my earthly temple there's a crowd;
There's one of us that's humble, one that's proud;
There's one that's brokenhearted for sins,
And one who, unrepentant, sits and grins;
There's one who loves his neighbor as himself,
And one who cares for naught but fame and self.
From such corroding care I would be free,
If once I could determine which is me.

-Unknown-

Understand yourself!

Discussion Questions

1. *How can understanding contribute to love?*
2. *What distinctive characteristic makes man different from the animals? Give scripture.*
3. *How is man the image of God?*
4. *What does the spirit contribute to the body?*
5. *What is the relationship of the body to the spirit as stated by Paul to the Corinthians?*
6. *Explain 1 John 2:16.*
7. *Is there any conflict between the spirit and the flesh? Explain.*
8. *How can such conflict be resolved?*
9. *Why is it important to resolve the conflict between the earth man and the spirit man?*
10. *What is essential to fulfillment in life?*

Chapter 3

FIND YOURSELF

The Romans had a saying for self-discovery, "Know Thyself."

A very godly man, a great gospel preacher, has well said, "Many lives are wasted in *purposeless living*." How many of us waste much of our lifetime before we *find* our purpose and place in life? Fortunate indeed is the individual who knows in youth what he wants in life and sets out to reach that goal.

Our Lord, in His Word, not only tells us *who* we are, but He gives us guidance into learning *what* we are.

In I Corinthians 12, Paul discusses a principle regarding the unity of the members of the body of Christ, which is His church. The body has many members which make up the body because each member has its necessary, individual function. If the foot should disclaim membership in the body because it is not the hand that does not make it any less a part of the body. If the whole body were an ear where would be the sense of smell, and if the whole body were an eye how would we hear? If all were a single organ there would be no body. God has arranged the organs in the body as He chose, giving *each its own function*, with each needing the other.

Some of the parts which seem inferior are given the greatest honor, and those parts we honor are least essential. Let us look at Phillips' translation: "Those parts of the body which have no obvious function are the more essential to health; and to those parts of the body which seem to us to be less deserving of notice we have to allow the highest honor of function. The parts which look beautiful may not be at all essential to life! But God has harmonized the whole body by giving importance of function to the parts which lack apparent importance, that the body should work together as a whole, with all the members in sympathetic relationship with one another."

This reminds us of Christ's teaching that the greatest would be he who was servant of all. (Matthew 23:11; Mark 9:35.)

The principle laid down by Paul must be applied to ourselves; each has a function in the body. Our task is to find ourselves, to learn what our function is, accept it, and perform it to the best of our ability.

Not all can be leaders; leaders must have followers and followers must have leaders. Not all can be in places of prominence. The work is usually done by the unsung heroes. Take a TV or movie star for example - where would the star be without the supporting cast, the costumer, the choreographer, the script writer, the cameraman, the lighting technician, etc., all of whom get a quick credit which flashes on the screen so fast it cannot be read.

In civic organizations there are those who get the glory, their names and pictures in the paper and the prominence, and there are the others who do the work! In business there are the administrators and the organizers who provide the jobs for the workers from foremen and block leaders to the janitors and maintenance personnel. Each is important in his function and necessary to keeping the business in harmonious operation.

God placed fathers, mothers, and children in the home unit, the father as the head of the home, the mother as the help meet, or the completion of the man, and children, who are to be obedient to these parents, "that it may be well with you and you may live long upon the earth." (Ephesians 6:1-3.)

In a recent article entitled "The Gifts of Solitude", Michael Drury states that solitude should not be jammed with busywork, but should be a time of introspection and self-renewal. As one young lady stated it, "I want to find out what I've got to offer me."

Find out what you have to offer yourself. If you are not an eye or a hand be content to be a little toe, or a spleen, or a nerve ending. If you are not a beautiful face be a red corpuscle which is necessary to make a face lovely. Who wants to do without these inferior parts of the body? I do not want to give up any part of my body, for each has its necessary function. Three years battle with pernicious anemia brings home the importance of good red blood cells for proper function of the body.

Do not underestimate yourself and your importance. There is a need for every individual and a place to fill. Find your function in life; be the best what-ever-you-are that you possibly can be. Be yourself! Do not try to be someone or something you are not. Do not try to be what you think others think you should be if it is contrary to what you are! Do not dissipate your energy and strength with frustrations and worries over your status in life. *Find yourself* and *be yourself*!

In an article in *Reader's Digest* by Terry A. Francois, a black man is telling his black brothers that the first responsibility of any individual is to find out *who* he is, and then to accept himself for *what* he is.

This leads us to our next facet of loving self, that is, to love ourselves we must accept ourselves.

Discussion Questions

1. *Who are you?*
2. *What is your goal in life?*
3. *What primary thing have you done to achieve that goal?*
4. *In 1 Corinthians 12:12-27 what is Paul saying to you?*
5. *What do you consider to be the most important member of your body?*
6. *Who is the most important member of the church?*
7. *Who is greatest according to Christ's teachings?*
8. *In the home unit what is your function?*
9. *What do you have to offer yourself?*
10. *Are you content with your status in life?*

Chapter 4

ACCEPT YOURSELF

A necessary part of finding oneself is accepting oneself. Let us again go to God's Word for guidance in what to accept in ourselves.

Not all can be men, nor can all be women. God saw the need for both and gave each his function. Not all can be adults, nor can all be teenagers, nor can all be children at will. Time determines which we are, just as it is determined at birth whether one is male or female. God created the man and the woman full grown adults and told them to multiply and fill the earth.

ACCEPT YOURSELF! If you are a *man* be a *man* and function in your God-given role as head of your household. Accept the God-given responsibility of providing for that household (I Timothy 5:8). Paul, through Jesus Christ, says you are worse than an infidel if you do not. Bring up your children in the nurture and admonition, or training, or discipline of the Lord (Ephesians 6:4). Note that this scripture specifies fathers are to do this. We hear much today about our matriarchal society and how mothers are responsible for all the homosexuals in today's society. Man can easily remedy this ill of society by accepting the above responsibility *instead of relegating it to the mother.*

Accept the responsibility of developing into spiritual leaders and qualifying as scriptural elders and deacons. If more elders were well-versed in the teaching of God's word (instead of not apt to teach if they can get out of it) the false teacher would never get his foot inside the door of the Lord's church.

Husbands, love your wives and do not be harsh with them (Colossians 3:19). Phillips reads, "be sure you give your wives love and sympathy; don't let bitterness or resentment spoil your marriage. Honor your wife" (I Peter 3:7). Learn to control your body, keeping it pure and treating it with respect, never regarding it as an instrument for self-gratification as the pagans who do not know God (I Thessalonians 4:4, 5). If you cannot control your body get married. God does not condone a double moral standard with license for immorality for the man. (Nor does He condone immorality for the woman.) Paul says in I Corinthians 7:2, because of the temptation to immorality let each man have his own wife and give her her conjugal rights.

ACCEPT YOURSELF! If you are a *woman* be a *woman*. Some of the most miserable people I know are women who wish they were men. They are filled with frustration, seeking "equal rights" with men and looking for fulfillment outside their God-given realm.

God created woman to be a wife and mother. In Genesis 1:28, after God made them male and female, He instructed them to be fruitful and multiply and fill the earth. The commission to procreate preceded the sin of the woman and the man. It is in error to teach or infer that child bearing is a penalty placed upon woman for sinning. God created her equipped to bear children; He did not have to do a quick remodeling job after the transgression.

Many women are so inhibited by this erroneous idea that they fail as wives. The wedding ceremony does not remove these inhibitions. Do not teach your daughter that it is wrong to give herself to the man she marries. *DO* teach your girls *and* your boys that they are to keep their bodies pure because immorality is forbidden by God and He is to be glorified in "your body". (I Corinthians 3:16,17; 6:18-20.) In I Corinthians 7:2 ff, God eliminates premarital sex by commanding every man to have his own wife and every woman to have her own husband in order to avoid fornication, or immorality. Each is to give the other his or her conjugal rights, not defrauding one another. A girl who is taught that "sex" is wrong because of fear of pregnancy will have difficulty in losing her inhibitions and giving her husband his conjugal rights. It can also mar her attitude toward her children. This has marred more than one marriage. Husband and wife are to refuse one another only by mutual consent and this is to be a temporary arrangement. Woman's body is not to be used as a weapon! "Love does not pursue selfish advantage."

When the woman sinned her penalty was two-fold; 1. she would have pain and travail in childbearing. Rachel travailed at the birth of Benjamin - she died in childbirth, in fact. Tamar travailed and gave birth to twins, sons of Judah, one of whom is named in the lineage of Christ. In John 16:21 Jesus says, "When a woman is in travail she has sorrow because her hour has come; but when she is delivered of the child she no longer remembers the anguish for joy that a child is born into the world."

2. Her husband will rule over her. There is probably more rebellion over this than any one thing. Some women read and resent Peter's statement in I Peter 3:7, that woman is the weaker sex and set about to prove him wrong by demanding equal rights with men. These completely overlook the statement of Peter declaring that the recognition of this fact demands honor from her husband! Let us read from Phillips' rendering of the passage: "Similarly, you husbands should try to understand the wives you live with, honoring them as physically weaker, yet equally heirs with you of the grace of life. If you don't do this you will find it impossible to pray properly."

Some have called Paul a woman hater, but he says he received his instructions through Jesus Christ, so do not blame Paul. In I Corinthians 11:3 we find that which can be called the "totem pole of authority".

GOD

The head of every man is - - - - ▶CHRIST
The head of a woman is - - - - - - - ▶HER HUSBAND
The head of Christ is - - ↗ GOD

This is God's way, and we will do well to accept it. Woman is prohibited from usurping authority over the man or dominating the man. (I Timothy 2:12) With authority goes responsibility, and woman should be "tickled to death" that God has given our men the responsibility of leadership. Go back and read the responsibilities God has put upon the man, then work to help and encourage your man to accept those responsibilities! It is easy for a woman to be in subjection to a man who is the kind of husband and father God requires him to be. Girls, let's let them have the authority!

ACCEPT YOURSELF! If you are a *teenager* accept yourself as being responsible to your parents. After Christ was twelve years old and had confounded the teachers in the temple with His questions and answers He returned to Nazareth with His mother and Joseph and was obedient to them. He spent His teenage years under their authority. (Luke 2:41-52.) He evidently learned the trade of Joseph, for His own countrymen asked, is not this the carpenter's son? (Matthew 13:55; Mark 6:3.) There was no communication gap between Jesus and Joseph in His teen years.

Disobedience to parents is called wickedness, classed in the same category with envy, murder, hatred of God; with the foolish, faithless, heartless, ruthless, who deserve to die. (Romans 1:28-32.)

You may know more about many things than your parents know, but *this does not give you license to disregard God's law to be subject to your parents and obey them*. Nor does it give you the wisdom and insight they may have gained with the years and experience. The wise teenager will accept himself, will follow Christ's example to be obedient to parents and will love and respect his parents. This is a service to God.

ACCEPT YOURSELF! Start *where* you are. Function to the best of your ability in your own realm.

Discussion Questions

1. *Who is the head of your household?*
2. *According to the scriptures:*
   a. *what are some responsibilties of the man?*
   b. *can a woman help her husband in his role of leadership?*
3. *Does God have a double standard of morality? Explain your answer.*
4. *Is child-bearing a penalty on woman? Explain.*
5. *What is wrong with pre-marital sex?*
6. *Is it all right for a woman to use her body as a weapon to get what she wants from her husband, or vice-versa?*
7. *When and why did woman lose her "equal rights"?*
8. *What is God's totem pole of authority?*
9. *Should teenagers be told by parents what they can and cannot do? Give scriptures.*
   a. *Who set an example of obedience to parents?*
   b. *In what category is disobedience to parents placed?*
10. *What is the first thing a teenager can do to serve God?*

Chapter 5

VALUE YOURSELF

It has been said that we are the result of our own choices; we are today where we *chose* to be! Our choices are determined by what we think of ourselves and our capabilities; hence, we are the fruit of our evaluation of ourselves.

Who are you?

All of us are part of God's creation, and everything that God had created was not only good, it was very good. (Genesis 1:31.) Every time we look into the mirror we should see ourselves as a creature of God and realize, "here is something that is good and it is my responsibility to take care of it." God did not run off a bunch of carbon copies in His creation. There are no identical fingerprints nor footprints. Every man, woman, and child is a distinct individual with individual identity, desires, and aspirations.

In Matthew 10:29-31, He reassured His disciples by saying that two sparrows were sold for a penny (not much value, money wise) yet God is aware when one falls to the ground. He feeds the birds that neither reap nor sow -. are we not of more value than they? God even knows how many hairs are on our heads! If He is that concerned about minute things in His creation how great must be His concern over man!!

What price would you put on your soul? For what price could you buy it back? In Matthew 16:26, Jesus asked what profit a man has if he gains the whole world and loses his soul; or what shall a man give in exchange for his soul? It is invaluable! It is from God! No matter how insignificant we may be in the eyes of men, nor how worthless we consider ourselves, God loves us because He made us, and to Him we are of such great value that He sent His only Son to earth to suffer death on a cross for us. How can one berate self and hate self when God loves him that much?

Women, if being low man on the totem pole makes you love yourself less, then you need to learn to value yourself. God created everything needed for the environment and welfare of man, then He created man from the dust of the ground. He planted a garden for the man and put him into this garden which was filled with every tree pleasant to the sight and good for food. In the midst of the garden were the tree of life and the tree of knowledge of good and evil. It was watered by a river with four tributaries. God put man there to till and keep the garden.

Seeing that it was not good for the man to be alone God brought all of the earth creatures to the man to be named, "but for the man there was not found a helper fit for him." So, the first anesthetic was administered, the first operation performed, and because of a specific need to be filled God made woman and brought her to the man to be a helper fit for him. The man's reaction was: "This at last, is bone of my bones and flesh of my flesh; she shall be called woman because she was taken out of man."

This woman was not made to be a help-meet, nor a help-mate, but a *helper fit for* the man. Paul says in I Corinthians 11:9, the woman was created for the man, and he explains this further in I Corinthians 15:39, when he says, "not all flesh is alike, but there is one kind for *men*, another for *animals*, another for *birds* and another for *fish*." What made the woman a helper fit for the man? The fact that she was bone of his bones, and flesh of his flesh, the female for the male!

Now the specific need had been filled, and God had created woman to fill it, not from the dust of the ground but from the man. It has been said that woman was created from finer material than the man; is there a man who will argue the point?

God placed the woman in her own domain, the home. The woman who is a homemaker is the queen of her realm. In defining the word home, Webster uses the word asylum. (Now, before you go into hysteria at the very thought of your home being an asylum for your husband and children, remember that Webster does not say "insane asylum".) Take a good look at the word asylum: 1. an inviolable sanctuary giving shelter; 2. any place of retreat and security; 3. protection provided by such sanctuary or place of retreat. Look at the definition again.

Is your home an inviolable sanctuary, a place of retreat and security for your family and yourself? If you are a homemaker what is the first thing your husband and children do when they come through the door? They locate the queen of their lives, right? They may be on the way to the refrigerator or out the back door to a hobby, but they make their presence known and locate the wife or mother if it is no more than waiting for a reply to "anybody home"?

Mrs. T. C. Clark, in her book, *Me and My House,* has stated the goal of the homemaker in this way: "To provide a place where the family's love of God may grow." To succeed in this she must value herself and her role with the proper perspectives which will promote her love of self.

The word picture of the worthy woman, recorded in Proverbs 31:10-31, is more or less familiar to all, but let us take another look at it. Examine it carefully for some of the traits of the worthy woman. She is

trustworthy,
loyal and faithful,
industrious,
well organized,
a good manager,
ambitious for her family,
healthy,
financially capable,
skillful,
charitable,
has vision and foresight,
she and her house are well groomed,
she honors her husband,
is resourceful and dignified, and
is a moral manager.

In despair you cry out, "Who can do all that?" YOU CAN. A homemaker *does.* The home has been described as the arena of life where woman can best use the talents God gave her. Where else but in the home can one find:

a dietician,
a chef,
a decorator,
a nurse,
a counselor,
a taxi-driver,
a tutor,
a seamstress,
a fashion model,
an entertainer,

a financial wizard,
a psychologist,
a personnel manager,
and LOVE,
all rolled into one person, wife and mother?

What is the reward? Her children rise up and call her blessed, and the king of her life says, "Many women have done excellently, but *you* surpass them all."

Low man on the totem pole, what is your worth? A worthy woman, who can find, for her price is far above rubies.

Second man on the totem pole, God entrusted this priceless person into your care and keeping with instructions to love her and honor her.

And God saw everything that He had created and behold, it was very good.

VALUE YOURSELF!

Discussion Questions

1. *What choices have you made that put you where you are today?*
2. *What is said of God's creation?*
3. *Are you a carbon copy? Explain.*
4. *Give a scripture that tells of God's concern for us.*
5. *Of what value is your soul?*
6. *Why was woman created?*
7. *In what realm is woman the queen?*
8. *What has been stated as the goal of the homemaker?*
9. *Name 10 traits of the worthy woman of Proverbs 31.*
   a. *Where can a woman best excel in the use of her talents?*
   b. *What is the reward of the worthy woman?*
10. *What great trust did God bestow upon the man?*

Chapter 6

RESPECT YOURSELF

It seems to be an innate characteristic of man to respect background and status. In introducing people we often hear, "he is the vice-president of Status Bank; she is the daughter of Prestige Family; her husband preaches for Big Name Church in Metropolis; or, they live on Elite Street in Sophistication Suburb." Most people feel respect for the so-called Upper Class, the Rich, and the Royalty of Society.

Part of Webster's definition of the word love is: a feeling of strong personal attachment induced by ties of kinship.

Do we, as Christians, realize what we have as ties of kinship? In addition to learning *who* we are, and accepting *what* we are, let us consider the great significance of *whose* we are.

The Lord instructed Paul to write in Ephesians 2:10, "For we are His workmanship, created in Christ Jesus for good works." Again, in Galatians 4:4-7, Paul writes that when the time was right God sent His Son that we might receive the *adoption* of sons and call God Father. We would not be *servants* but *children,* elevated in station from a *slave* in bondage to an *heir* with God's own Son.

Paul tells the Romans in chapter 8 that those who walk according to the dictates of the spirit man instead of the earth man are children of God, heirs of God, and joint-heirs with Christ. He continues with the assuring statement that NO THING AND NO ONE can separate us from the love of God. Only we, ourselves, can separate ourselves from God, if we fail to remember our ties of kinship and are disobedient to God's will. Being aware of *whose* we are we will love our Father, eagerly learning what He wants us to do and doing it.

What does it mean to be a child of God and a joint-heir with Christ? It means that I have a father-son relationship with God, and that assures me that He and His Son will be living with me. (John 14:23.) It means having the protection of a loving father who shields his child from harm. If God be for us who can be against us? (Romans 8:31.) It means I have a Father who disciplines me for my own good, not just for His own pleasure and to get it out of His system, as earthly fathers sometimes do. (Hebrews 12:5-11.) Verse 8 states that one who is not disciplined by the Father is not a *son*, but a *bastard*! His discipline assures me of being His child. This is not to be interpreted to mean that all problems and discomforts are from God, and that the more we are in trouble the more assured we can be that we are His children. The same scripture that tells us we are joint-heirs with Christ states the condition of that relationship; we are children and heirs IF WE SUFFER WITH HIM, in order that we may also be glorified with Him. (Romans 8:17.) Peter tells Christians not to be ashamed of suffering as a Christian but to glorify God *in that name*. He also says that if one suffers as a thief or murderer, as a wrong-doer or a mischief maker he is getting what he deserves and there is no glory in that. (I Peter 4:12-16.)

To have Christ live with me means I have the influence of One who has experienced the same problems I face, (He was tempted in every way man is tempted, yet without sin, Hebrews 4:15); One who will bridge the communication gap between me and my Father. (I Timothy 2:5.) I have access to a power so great that it raised Jesus from the grave and assures me of more than this life has to offer. It assures me of a love that is so long, so high, so wide, and so deep that it cannot be comprehended. (Ephesians 3:18, 19) As recorded in Ephesians 1:16-20, Paul prays that God would give the Christians at Ephesus the wisdom and insight to realize the *extensive riches and tremendous power* that were theirs.

Much of man's time and energy today is directed toward achieving riches and power when both are at the very fingertip of the child of God. In Ephesians 3:20, 21, Paul states that we have a Father who is able to do more than we can even think about or ask for. Child of the most powerful and richest king, member of the most royal family existing, respect yourself.

Most people observed via satellite the investiture of Prince Charles as the Prince of Wales, and anticipate his coronation as king of England at some future date. Much of the ritual seemed tedious and meaningless to us, and evidently required much study and concerted effort from him. Yet, in its glory and pomp was anyone heard to say it was unnecessary and foolish and should have been eliminated? Would any have advocated that the young prince should have rebelled at the demands of the ritual, embarrassed and shamed his mother through disobedience to the demands of the honor and yet received his crown? Was there anyone who was not impressed with the beauty and the riches of the robe and sceptre?

Did not all of us secretly yearn to be a part of such a heralded and colorful event? Yet, we fail to respect ourselves as part of a royal court much richer and more powerful than that could ever be, a court which is not limited to one crown, but one which has a crown for each one who will conform to the rules and regulations and will wear the royal robes of righteousness (II Timothy 4:8; I Peter 5:4; Revelation 2:10).

A child of the king will show self-respect by being well-groomed in the Lord (I Peter 3:3-6). As children of God we are part of the bride of Christ, and the bride arrays herself in fine linen, pure and white. What self-respecting person would be guilty of soiling his bridal attire? John writes in Revelation 19:8, that the fine linen, pure and white, is the righteous deeds of the saints. Royalty does not drag the royal robes, nor the royal name, through the muck and mire of immorality. "Love has good manners (is not rude)."

There is an incident told of one of the late, well-known, greatly loved preachers—he had glistening white hair, was short of stature, and always wore a confident smile. One day a gentleman remarked to him, "Brother ________, you act like you own the whole world", to which he smilingly replied, "My Father does!"

Remember whose you are! You are a chosen race, a royal priesthood, a holy nation, God's own people, a kingdom of priests who shall reign as kings upon the earth (I Peter 2:9; Revelation 5:10).

RESPECT YOURSELF!

Discussion Questions

1. *Are you concerned with status?*
2. *Quote Ephesians 2:10.*
3. *Are you a slave?*
4. *How much does Christianity elevate us?*
5. *Name some benefits you are enjoying because of this kinship with Christ.*
6. *What does Hebrews 12:5-11 mean to you? Write it in your own words.*
7. *Are you benefitting from the influence of our Older Brother?*
8. *How are you taking advantage of the riches and power that are availble to you*
9. *Decribe your royal robe.*
10. *Whose are you?*

Chapter 7

ENJOY YOURSELF

One facet of love as defined by Webster is "to take delight in." Once we really realize who we are, what we are, and whose we are, we are in a position to enjoy ourselves.

There is a well-worn story about the little boy who looked at the sad-faced mule hanging his head over the fence and said to his grandfather, "That old mule must be a Christian." When asked why he drew that conclusion he replied, "Because he has such a long face."

A stoic or pious look does not insure the righteousness of the wearer. Rather than *give* the impression of Christianity that the little boy had formed we should *live* the impression that Christians are the happiest people in the world.

The writer was loaned a book by a neighbor, *Search For Serenity,* a book used by Alcoholics Anonymous. In it is the statement, Misery is optional.

Misery is optional! This struck a full-faced blow. What does God say about this? Previously, much study had been done on a lesson on being happy. In running references on the word happy, one reads:

> Happy is the man whom God reproves: therefore, despise not the *chastening* of the Lord (Job 5:7).
>
> You shall eat the fruit of the *labor of your hands* and you shall be happy (Psalm 128:2).
>
> Paul said he was happy to be called before Agrippa to *defend himself* against the accusations of the Jews (Acts 26:2).
>
> Peter wrote, if you *suffer* for righteousness sake you will be happy (I Peter 3:14).
>
> If you are *reproached* for the name of Christ you are happy (I Peter 4:14).

Now, wait a minute! Happiness is connected with *being chastened*, with *working to eat, defending self against false accusers*, etc. Was the little boy so far wrong then?

Yes, he was wrong. Bible happiness is synonymous with blessedness, and is summed up by David in Psalm 144:15, "Happy the people whose God is the Lord." Solomon said, "Happy is he who finds wisdom and gets understanding."

This is not exactly what we have in mind, usually, when we

think of happiness. The word happy is defined: favored by hap, luck, or fortune, and the synonym is lucky. Most of us are looking for luck instead of real enjoyment.

The Declaration of Independence guarantees the right to the pursuit of happiness, and we continually pursue it. If misery is optional and I am miserable in my pursuit for happiness, then I had better take a good look at me.

To rejoice is a command, given not once, but many times. It is just as important to keep this command as it is to forsake not the assembling of yourselves together, to be baptized into Christ, or to love one another. Yet, how many times have you heard a lesson or a sermon on the command to rejoice, and to be happy and content?

The first meaning of the word rejoice is to *give joy*, to *gladden*. This is contrary to our way of thinking. To enjoy self, to us, actually means being the recipients of joy and gladness rather than being responsible for giving joy to or gladdening the hearts of others. We want the old "Eat, drink, and be merry" kind of enjoyment. *Have fun* is the watchword for today's society.

This outlook is confusing *pleasure* with happiness. Pleasure can be bought; happiness cannot be. In Romans 14:17 Paul expresses it, "the kingdom of heaven is not a matter of whether you get what you like to eat and drink, but of righteousness and peace and joy in the Holy Spirit."

Our fun-oriented world and our search for happiness explains today's money madness, the drive for pleasures that can be bought, not realizing that *no one, no place, no thing* can make us happy. Happiness is our option, and it comes from within. It is determined by our attitudes and our reactions toward circumstances.

A well-known psychiatrist who is also a Christian has stated that a high percentage of unhappiness comes from fear of our peers, of what others think of us. Many of our actions are governed by this fear. We make ourselves miserable worrying about what others think of us when all of the time they are thinking of themselves, too. Our concern should be, "What does God think of me?", and "What do I think of myself?" Do we forget, or have we not learned Romans 8:31 and Hebrews 13:6? He has promised, "I will never leave thee nor forsake thee," hence we can confidently say, "The Lord is my helper, I will not be afraid. What can man do to me?"

Paul told Timothy that godliness with contentment is great gain (I Timothy 6:6). Too many people have just enough fear of God to make them miserable, but not enough love to make serving Him enjoyable. Which do I opt to do — enjoy serving God because of the joy set before me, or feel deprived and imposed upon because of my feeble efforts? Do I choose to want a new car, a new house, a new fur, etc. like the Sophisticates down the street, or do I choose to be thankful for a roof over by head, the comforts of weather conditioning, and a full freezer and pantry?

Consider: What do you have to offer you? Edgar A. Guest wrote a poem that is expressive of this thought:

I have to live with myself, and so
I want to be fit for myself to know.

One definition of enjoy is to have possession or use of, to have the benefit of. To enjoy oneself one must love oneself and have the mastery of self to choose between pleasure and happiness.

Misery is Optional.

Rejoice evermore.

ENJOY YOURSELF.

Discussion Questions

1. *Are you happy? If so, have you notified your face?*
2. *Define happiness as presented in the Bible.*
3. *Give 3 scriptures that command us to rejoice or be joyful.*
4. *Define the word rejoice.*
5. *With what do we often confuse happiness?*
6. *what causes a high percentage of unhappiness?*
7. *Write out Romans 8:31.*
8. *What does Hebrews 13:5-6 mean to you?*
9. *Do you believe that misery is optional?*
10. *What will make you happy?*

Chapter 8

FORGIVE YOURSELF

To be more fit to live with and to attain the enjoyment the Christian life offers one must be able to forgive oneself. In Leviticus 19:17, 18, God told His people not

to hate,
to take vengeance, nor
to bear a grudge

against their neighbors, but to love one's neighbor as himself. If loving one's neighbor involves these three things then it follows that to love oneself one must not hate himself, nor take vengeance on himself, nor bear any grudge against himself.

Who among us has not hated himself for something he has done, and has tossed, turned, lost sleep, and grieved over an act or a hasty word, when what he really needed to do was ask God's forgiveness, forgive himself and forget it? Do not bear a grudge against yourself.

Jesus taught His disciples to pray to God to forgive them as they forgave others. In Luke 6:37, He taught, "forgive and it will be forgiven you." Most of this teaching involves forgiving others, but is it not probable that our difficulty in forgiving others hinges on our inability to forgive self? Do we not believe that God forgives us when we ask Him to do so? Then why do we go over again and rehash all the lurid details of our failings and transgressions, repeatedly torturing ourselves instead of forgiving ourselves in the same way we expect God to forgive us?

There are times when we just do not like ourselves. Medical science has determined that many so-called accidental deaths are actually suicides, people who dislike themselves to the point of carelessness, even daring, with their own lives. They become so self-consumed that they drive on the wrong side of the road, or do other suicidal things.

Let us look at two Bible characters who struggled with the problem of forgiving themselves. In Matthew 26 we see two of the disciples of Jesus, Judas, who conspired to sell our Lord for thirty pieces of silver, and Peter, who confidently stated he would never be offended because of Christ and was ready to die for Him. Before the night was over Judas had tried to return the blood money to those who had paid him to betray the Lord. Not stopping with this act he even repented, Matthew tells us.

But what did he do about it? He went out and hanged himself.

Did self-confident Peter go to death with his Lord? No, he denied that he knew Him. Matthew says he cursed and swore, saying he did not know the man. The rooster's crowing reminded Peter of his pledged allegiance, and his Master's having predicted that Peter would deny Him. The Lord looked at Peter, a reminder to him of His awareness of what had happened. How did Peter handle the situation? He wept bitterly, remorsefully. Did Peter bury himself in this grief and remorse, becoming useless to the Master? No, we find him back with his nets on an unsuccessful fishing expedition when Jesus, the risen Christ, appeared to Peter and the others, and He asked Peter three times, "Peter, do you love me?" This same Peter preached the first gospel sermon, opening the doors of the kingdom the Lord said He would build.

God told His people, "You shall not stand against the life of your neighbor." One who loves himself as he is told to love his neighbor will forgive himself of his follies and will not stand against his own life.

People who do not forgive themselves often avenge themselves by abusing their minds and bodies with harmful habits. Some overeat and get fatter and fatter. Some turn to alcohol or narcotics. Some develop persecution complexes or become self-made martyrs. Some steal, subconsciously hoping to get caught and be punished. Some become pathological liars, or numerous other things that could be named. They cannot forgive themselves for missing the mark they want for themselves.

It has been stated that forty-three percent of all psychiatric cases are people who harbor a guilt complex and cannot forgive themselves. Guilt feelings destroy our good will toward self. Webster defines love as a strong liking, fondness, good will. To destroy one's good will to self is to destroy one's love for self.

Paul told Timothy to hold on to his faith and a good conscience. (I Timothy 1:19.) Peter wrote to Christians to keep a clear conscience so that when they were abused their revilers would be put to shame. One can give the best of himself only when he is not frustrated and dissipated with guilt. Paul said he had always acted in good conscience. Even when he was persecuting Christians, even putting them to death, he did it with the right motive because his conscience had been educated to keep the law of Moses. As soon as he was shown that he was wrong he gave up his old ways and started over. Paul had much to forgive in himself, yet he did not dissipate his energy and usefulness in remorse and self-deprecation, nor fill his writings with apologies or excuses.

What was Paul's formula for a clear conscience? He gives it in Philippians 3:13,14 - *forgetting what lies behind and looking forward,* pressing on to the goal of the high calling in Christ Jesus. Christ said He came to the sinners, not to the righteous. No sin is too big to be forgiven.

Making sure our conscience is clear entails forgetting the past and forgiving self. Webster defines forgive: to give up resentment against or the desire to punish. Love does not keep account of evil. God promises to *remember no more* the sins that He forgives. Do not mess up today by looking backward to yesterday! (Luke 9:67.) Look forward.

Forgive yourself and forget it!

Discussion Questions

1. *In Leviticus 19:17-18 what did God tell His people about hate and vengeance?*
2. *Have you ever held a grudge against yourself?*
3. *Do you believe God forgives you? (When He forgives what else does He do?)*
4. *How did Judas handle forgiving himself?*
5. *How did peter handle the problem of forgiving himself?*
6. *What will guilt feelings do for one?*
7. *Write I Peter 3:15-16 in your own words. What does it say about conscience?*
8. *What formula did Paul use for a clear conscience?*
9. *What is Webster's definition of the word forgive?*
10. *Have you forgiven yourself, getting rid of all resentment and guilt feelings?*

Chapter 9

BE PATIENT WITH YOURSELF

"Love is patient." Paul puts patience at the head of the list of attributes of love. (I Corinthians 13:4.) To love oneself is to learn to be patient with oneself.

According to Webster patient is: 1. enduring pain, trouble, etc., with composure and without complaining; 2. refusing to be provoked, as by an insult; 3. calmly tolerating delay, confusion, etc.

Perhaps the best place to start in developing patience with self is to recognize one's limitations. That we have limitations is taught by Christ in His parable of the talents. Here we need to use a positive approach with self by eliminating the negative, the I-am-nots, and the I-do-nots! Again, we are the result of our own choices; no one can make you feel inferior unless you yourself cooperate.

This has been well said in a recent publication, "Do not be guilt ridden because of a feeling of inadequacy; the great gulf between what you are and what you feel you should be." It is all right to hitch your wagon to a star if you are content to be earthbound. Many times this gap between what we feel we are and what we feel we should be is made evident by a brash, boastful, rubberarm attitude. A sarcastic, overly critical personality often says that the individual carries a feeling of inadequacy and is impatient with self. Instead of a calm, *unhurried approach* to self there is an *impatient reproach* of self covered up with apparent ego.

In "Power For Today", Neil Lightfoot has quoted the words of a song, One Step At A Time, applying them to the progressive growth of a Christian. We are limited to one step at a time in whatever we undertake. He continues, "How many times we falter and fail! We are disappointed and discouraged almost daily. Do these things happen because we try to advance too rapidly? Yes! We expect to take giant steps and when we fail we blame ourselves or God." We must be patient enough to take small, faltering steps until we reach a firm footing, and even then it is necessary to keep a constant vigil on our path.

Each person has *physical limitations.* This necessitates the weighing of values and abilities. One may be better able to accept his limitations if he recognizes and honors his realm of responsibility. The area of authority and responsibility was presented in Chapter 4. When each person recognizes and operates within the limitations of his own responsibility his sense of attainment will be greater and he will feel less impatient with self. Much of the frustration of the times is a result of some who do not accept their responsibilities, so others step outside their own realm trying to take care of the responsibilities that are being neglected. Be it the home, business, church, or nation, for a smooth operation it is essential that "every member perform its own function".

No person can be all the places doing all the things that need to be done all of the time. This is why we are taught that each member has a function and each must do its part to keep the body serving its purpose. Our task is to find our area of service and function in that capacity with composure and without complaining.

Christ did not heal every case of physical illness, even though He cured many, (immediately and without relapse!). He did not secure equal job opportunity for all men, nor did He guarantee an annual wage. He helped the fishermen catch more fish than their nets would hold, and He paid taxes to Caesar. Christ, being divine, was not limited as we are but *He limited Himself to doing the work of God.* He left undone many of the things we try to do, yet He did the will of His Father, and Glorified His Father by doing the work He was sent to do. (John 17: 4.) He worked in His own realm of responsibility.

To follow His example is to evaluate the things put before us and make proper choices. This requires a constant two-way communication with God, a study of His word, daily, and daily prayer to Him.

The personal hang-up of this writer was the command to teach the whole world. This weighed heavily and caused concern with numbers - to teach as many people as possible in as many classes as possible, was the goal set to be reached. The result was energy expended in begging people who claimed to be God's children to come study His word which they themselves should have been teaching to others, people described in Hebrews 5:12,13.

Then came the dawn! Jesus calmly taught one woman, a willing, uncoerced listener at a well, and the whole city came out to hear. Jesus taught twelve selected men carefully and thoroughly, then commissioned them to teach the whole world by *teaching the taught ones to teach others.*

We are hangers-on, wanting to see a person converted before we leave him. We want to do the planting, watering, and harvesting at one sitting. We do not have the patience to take one step at a time. Jesus and the apostles taught the Word, then left the individual with the free choice of accepting or rejecting it. The Father seeks *worshippers,* (John 4:23), *not coerced followers.* The responsibility of accepting the Word after it is taught is an individual responsibility and God is the judge.

When this writer quit the formal classroom and let God do the leading He opened doors that this limited vision would never have seen. It is really amazing how many people are truly interested in hearing about God when we get outside of what we call the brotherhood!

To be patient with self requires the ability to know when one is making undue demands on self. One cannot please all of the people all of the time; in fact, one cannot please some people any of the time! Earn the respect of others by developing the ornament of a quiet and meek spirit. This requires patience - the will and the ability to endure without complaint. The author has spent years endeavoring to "study to be quiet and to do your own business". This has required (and still requires) the ultimate in calm toleration of self.

Another area where patience with self is required is bridling the tongue. Much pain, trouble, sorrow, etc. has to be endured because of the failure to bridle the tongue. Instead of refusing to be provoked often our reaction is completely opposite. Our intentions are good, and we tell ourselves we will hold our tongues, then before we know it a fire has been kindled. It is true that James says the tongue can not be tamed, but *that is no excuse for putting away the bridle!*

In one place patience is defined thus: expectant with calmness, without discontent, undisturbed by obstacles, delays, failures. "Don't worry at all then about tomorrow. Tomorrow can take care of itself! One day's trouble is enough for one day." (Matthew 6:34.)

BE PATIENT WITH YOURSELF!

Discussion Questions

1. *What is the first attribute of love named by Paul in the love chapter, I Corinthians 13?*
2. *How does Webster define the word patient?*
3. *What will help in developing patience with self?*
4. *How important is patience? Luke 21:19.*
5. *Do you feel that limitations are a weakness?*
6. *What limitation did Christ place upon Himself?*
7. *Do you make undue demands on yourself?*
8. *In what area do you need to develop patience with yourself?*
9. *Quote Matthew 6:34.*
10. *What is your area of responsibility?*

Chapter 10

BE HONEST WITH YOURSELF

In Exodus 20:16, God tells Israel they are not to bear false witness against their neighbor. Paul admonishes the brethren in Ephesians 4:25, to put away falsehood and speak the truth with his neighbor. You may ask, "How does this apply to my loving myself?"

A much respected preacher has said, "We must tell ourselves the truth—be truthful with ourselves—not lying to ourselves about ourselves. Jesus said, 'The truth will make you free!' That can be applied here. We talk much about the sin of lying, then lie *to* ourselves *about* ourselves and go unhappily on our way. Only when we face up to ourselves can we be free and happy."

How can one be guilty of bearing false witness against himself? John states that if we say we have no sin we deceive ourselves and the truth is not in us. "Oh, but no one would say he has no sin!" Are you sure? It is easy enough to admit that one misses the mark—after all—Paul said in Romans that all have sinned and come short of the glory of God. Let us take a look at some of the "missing the mark" to which we may not face up.

Will one admit to having a double standard, one for THEE and one for ME? When THEE is late to an appointment THEE is undependable, but if ME is late ME is providentially hindered. If the preacher pours it on THEE for going out of town to the sports event Saturday night and being late to Bible school Sunday morning he is really a fine preacher, but if he touches on ME for playing "42", or Bridge until the wee hours and missing Bible school he is meddling. THEE wastes time watching television while ME improves (?) self by reading all of the latest philosophical tripe.

Paul had something to say about this double standard in Romans 2:21ff, asking, you who teach others, do you teach yourself? Do you teach against stealing and then steal (pad the expense account, cheat on your income tax return, keep the overpayment in change), do you teach against committing adultery, then commit adultery, do you abhor idols then rob temples? Do you make excuses for things you do which you do not tolerate in others? In other words, do you practice what you preach?

Face yourself! Why are you so angry with Sister Missionary? Is it because of your own shortcomings and you cannot admit to being angry with yourself so you take it out on her? Why does deacon No. 1 get so angry when deacon No. 2 gets glory for doing less than deacon No. 1 is doing? Is No. 1 serving for honor from men or for approval from God? I cannot like Mr. Studious for a teacher. Why? Is he smarter than I or am I just lazier than he? I'm better than Mr. Scoundrel any day! In all honesty, why compare self with the little man? Why not take Mr. Uprightman for our comparison?

Examine self, Paul says (II Corinthians 13:5). Examine motives and attitudes. Be honest with self. Why do I want to teach this class, make this talk, attend this meeting? Must I always be right, regardless of the error of which I may be guilty? Love is glad when truth prevails. Do I love myself enough to be honest and yield my stand to let truth prevail? It is a sad truth that too many people prefer to see experiments hindered, projects abandoned, and progress impeded rather than honestly allowing Truth to prevail!

How many will admit the sin of envy, of false pride; or how many will be honest with self in examining motives prompting certain criticisms and judgments; or who will admit to the sin of judging? How many are willing to disagree without being disagreeable?

Why does one gloat over the wickedness of others? Can one elevate himself by cutting down others? The individual who bitterly denounces others in his field needs to *reason with himself* and find out why he tears down instead of builds up. The militant radical who rebels against the establishment by destroying what he does not like will awaken someday to find that all he has to offer his children is a destroyed establishment, a pile of charred ruins and lawless chaos. It has been said one dog barks at the moon and the other dogs bark at the noise! We have a lot of barking done today from individuals who do not know what the noise is all about!

Let us not be victims of our own self-deceit. Let us honestly face up to our shortcomings and try to remedy them. James says the man who thinks he is religious and bridles not his tongue deceives himself. Jesus taught that out of the heart a man speaks, and by his words he will be either justified or condemned (Matthew 12:34, 37). Solomon stated that man is what he thinks—"as he thinketh in his heart, so is he" (Proverbs 23: 7, KJV). Paul taught the Corinthians that thoughts need to be captured and brought under control (II Corinthians 10:5).

Recently, in a conversation about proper diet and weight control a man said, "I have learned that in order to change my eating habits I have to change the way I think." This is a very profound insight. To change any habit it is necessary to change the way one thinks. To bridle the tongue one must capture his thoughts and change his way of thinking. Paul wrote Timothy that the aim of their charge "is love that issues from a pure heart and a good conscience and sincere faith" (I Timothy 1:5). He told the Philippians to "fix your minds" (capture your thoughts) on whatever is pure and honorable and just and true and lovely and praiseworthy (Philippians 4:8, Phillips). This requires honesty with self.

It is possible to examine self and yet not face oneself. The prodigal son *came to himself* (came to his senses, v. 17, NEB and Phillips), faced himself in his true situation and remedied it (Luke 15:11ff). He was honest with himself.

In being honest with self there is no room for sham. *Love does not try to impress.* One who is honest with self will not try to be, nor try to impress others, that he is something which he is not. Miniskirts are not for grandmothers! Artificially coloring one's hair to keep it the same color it was in one's youth only hardens the features of an older person and deepens the lines of time on one's face. Shams add to one's insecurity. Recently in a situation comedy an older man was trying to impress a young secretary with his youth and agility. He discarded his glasses for contact lenses, dressed youthfully, and took her to one of the "in" places. While doing a mod dance he lost his contact lenses and, of course, made a complete fool of himself. The *uncomical* thing about it all is that too many people in real life embarrass themselves and others by being dishonest with selves and trying to impress others that they are something they are not.

Shakespeare said it well in *Hamlet*, Act 1, scene 3:

This above all: to thine own self be true,
and it must follow, as the night the day,
thou canst not then be false to any man.

BE HONEST WITH YOURSELF!

Discussion Questions

1. *Why is it important to be honest with ourselves about ourselves?*
2 *How can being truthful with self promote freedom in our lives?*
3. *Is it easy for you to name your sins and admit them?*
4. *Relate a scripture that deals with a double standard for self.*
5. *After self-examination state to yourself what you have learned about yourself*
6. *How would you rate your self-image? Why?*
7. *What determines what a person really is? Give scripture.*
8. *To change self what must first be changed?*
9. *Do you allow sham to have a place in you life?*
10. *Explain honesty-with-self as stated by shakespeare.*

Chapter 11

WASTE NOT YOURSELF

It has been said, "You cannot waste time for time is always here, neither more nor less, and always moving at a steady pace. When you do not use time to the best possible advantage to yourself, to society, to God, you are wasting yourself."

Paul wrote the Ephesians in 5:15, 16, look carefully how you walk; walk wisely, not unwisely, making the most of your time (redeeming the time, KJV). *How one's time is spent determines how oneself is spent.*

In I John 4:18, the disciple whom Jesus loved tells us that there is no fear in love, but perfect love casts out fear. One who loves himself will not waste himself with time spent in fear. We fear what our peers think of us. We fear what our children think of us. We fear what our in-laws (and out-laws) think of us. This fear often leads to self-pity. Some even *enjoy* feeling sorry for themselves and bask in imagining all sorts of slights, innuendos, and hardships.

Here, again, it is necessary to *capture* our thoughts. Why waste thoughts which run helter-skelter, without organization? Give conscious effort to controlling your thought pattern and notice how far afield it goes if not captured. When *captured and encased* in things that are pure, lovely, just, true, and of good report, self-pity goes out the window and one is no longer a victim of his fears of his peers.

Another fear to be cast out by loving self is lack of self-trust, an insecurity that causes much waste of self. Mr. Samuel Goldwyn, the successful motion picture producer, states that years ago he came to the conclusion that when one looks to others for security he is looking in the wrong direction. To quote him: "The greatest security a person can have comes from within himself, not from the outside. Nothing can match what you can do for yourself." He closes with this advice to young people (and it applies to all ages), "Don't dream about security—make it for yourself, out of yourself. Dare to believe in yourself and act accordingly." Emerson said, "Self-trust is the first secret of success." When one understands, accepts, respects, and loves himself as a creature of God and as His child he will not waste himself with insecurity.

Do not waste yourself with busyness. This is a busy age.

We take our children to psychiatrists if they persist in daydreaming. We do not allow them to lie down on the grass and watch the clouds form great masterpieces. They are not allowed to develop the creativity of imagination; they are either accused of lying or are grabbed up and taken to band practice, Little League, Pop Warner football practice, to Scouts, etc., etc., etc.

We either take tranquilizers or go to the psychiatrist (or both) ourselves because of nervous frustrations resulting from our busyness. It is necessary to evaluate our activities and make some choices.

One Christian woman, well known in her community for her good works, may have misplaced her values. There was never a death nor an illness, nor any other need in the community, that she was not there assisting in every way possible. She taught school and told her pupils about God; she taught Bible classes in the Sunday School, and conducted personal work classes. But—in her home was an unbelieving husband, and of the six children raised in that home not one makes any profession of being a Christian.

Let us again refer to Mrs. Clark's statement of the ultimate goal of the homemaker, *"To provide a place where the family's love of God may grow."* If we taught all of our own children to be followers of Christ the church of the Lord would more than double in size in a generation.

In a tight situation God told Moses to *stand still*. It could be an interesting exercise to study how many times God told His people to be still. In Psalm 46:10, He told David to "Be still and know that I am God." So much happiness is lost in haste.

In a recent issue of *Family Weekly* (also reprinted in *Reader's Digest*) there is an article entitled "You Are Shaping Your Children's Memories". The author asked his son what he remembered best and without hesitation he replied, "The night we were driving somewhere on a dark road and you stopped the car and helped me catch fireflies." The author then relates the incident which he had forgotten. When he asked his son why he remembered that incident he received the answer, "Maybe it was because I didn't think you were going to stop and catch any for me—and then you did."

This caused the writer to stop and remember a best moment in her own childhood. Often the trip was made from West Texas to the Lower Rio Grande Valley. Always it was a matter of seeing how short a time it would take to make the trip. Then one glorious day my father stopped the car and took time to take me down to a railroad tunnel under the highway between Fredericksburg and Waring. Oh, what a great experience that was! Though the highway has bypassed Waring for many years now and the train stopped long ago, I am told that the tunnel is still in existence and some day I shall *take time* to visit it again.

These thoughts called to mind an incident a friend had told of a memory expressed by her own child. During the hard times many of us knew, they had been traveling and out of necessity had stopped, made a fire, and cooked their breakfast by the side of the road. The child was not aware of the necessity—only of the happy breakfast beside the road, a family sharing!

In I Kings 20:35ff we read a parable which is applicable to today's way of life. A servant was entrusted with the keeping of a war hostage taken in battle, a trust which required the life of the servant if he failed it. Verse 40 states, "And as your servant was busy here and there, he was gone." The servant accepted the trust with full realization of his responsibility; he was not indifferent to it, nor was he idle; he failed his trust by being *consumed with busyness.* Parents are failing their trust with their children, at the risk of their eternal lives, by being too busy to nurture their children in the Lord's admonition. Men and women are too busy to give their own eternal status proper time and thought. "As your servant was busy here and there, he was gone."

If I love myself I will not waste myself and my children and grandchildren with busyness. I will not waste myself with frustrations that absorb my energy and time, frustrations of self-pity and insecurity.

If I love myself I will walk wisely, making the most of my time.

WASTE NOT YOURSELF!

Discussion Questions

1. *Memorize Ephesians 5:15-16.*
2. *What determines how one spends self?*
3. *How and why is fear harmful?*
4. *Explain "capture your thoughts".*
5. *Why should one trust self?*
6. *How busy are your days? List your activities.*
   - a . *What does your busyness accomplish for you?*
   - b . *do you have time to get better acquainted with God?*
   - c . *Quote Psalm 46:10; explain what it means to you.*
7. *What is your most pleasant childhood memory with a parent? Did it involve money or time or both?*
8. *Tell the story of the servant of I Kings 20:35ff.*
   - a . *Did he understand his responsibility?*
   - b . *What caused his failure?*
9. *Name the two top priorities on your time.*
10. *How much time do you allow for standing still with God?*

Chapter 12

HURT NOT YOURSELF

Love hurts no one. (Romans 13:10, Phillips.) One who loves himself will not hurt himself.

Love does not try to impress. This is a time when men are seeking knowledge. Like the Athenians in Acts 17, men are spending their time hearing or telling of some new thing. It is an age of sophistication, and many are trying to impress the world with how much they know. Preachers quote Hebrew, Aramaic and Greek trying to impress their hearers that they are superior in knowledge and understanding; yet their daily application of Bible principles proves that they are carried away with their own sophistication. Youth tries to impress the world with their worldly wisdom, so they learn to smoke and drink, use worldly language, and dress, or undress, in the latest fads.

What is sophistication? Let us look at some definitions:

Sophisticate — to disillusion; to make worldly use; to deprive of genuineness, naturalness, simplicity.

sophisticated — made artificial, highly complicated, worldly wise.

sophistication — sophistry, sophistical reasoning, state of being sophisticated.

sophistry — sophistical or deceptively subtle reasoning or argumentation.

Paul told the Colossians to beware of philosophy and vain deceit of men. Phillips calls it intellectualism and high sounding nonsense. To the Corinthians he wrote, "If anyone thinks he is wise let him become a fool so he can become wise. Wisdom of this world is folly with God."

The writer first became interested in the true meaning of sophistication after reading a little book by Archibald Rutledge, *Life's Extras*. In it he states, "I have the gravest suspicions of sophistication. I have never discovered it in nature".

According to the definitions given, sophistication is artificial, disillusioning, void of genuineness. Perhaps this explains why some of the people who were most sophisticated have taken their own lives, and others have committed slow suicide by resorting to alcoholism, narcotics and dissipation of various sorts, because of their unfulfilled lives.

Love does not try to impress; love builds up. If I love myself I will not hurt myself with sophistication.

If I love myself I will not hurt myself with self-conceit. "Love does not cherish inflated ideas of its own importance." This makes the premise of this book seem paradoxical, does it not? How do we reconcile "Love Yourself" with such scriptures as Romans 12:3, "I bid a man not to think more highly of himself than he ought to think"; and Galatians 6:3, "if a man thinks himself to be something, when he is nothing, he deceives himself".

Self-conceit is: overweening opinion of one's powers, vanity, excessive self-importance; exaggerated; egotistic, arrogant. In Galatians 5:26, Paul writes, "Let us have no self-conceit, no provoking of one another, no envy of one another". Paul describes the latter in his second letter to Timothy in 3:1-5. He catalogs quite a list of descriptive terms applying them to men who are lovers of self, and gets to the real crux of the matter in v. 4 when he says their *love of pleasure* is greater than their *love of God*. This self-conceit which is condemned and forbidden is the exaggerated opinion one has of his ability to attain stature without God's help. *Herein lies the error.*

This again points out the dual nature of man, and the *self* referred to in the above scriptures is the *earth* man. Recognition of dependence upon God is part of loving self. Recognition of our relationship as co-laborers with God increases our self-respect and that of our neighbor. To conquer the desires of the *earth* man and bring him into subjection to the *spirit* man requires a realization of one's dependence and reliance on God. Taking partnership with God could end all of society's ills.

If I love myself I will not think more highly of myself than I ought to think; I will not deceive myself by thinking I am something when, without God, I am nothing; I will not love pleasure more than I love God.

If I love myself I will not hurt myself with intemperance. The definition of the word is: lack of moderation or restraint; excessive; over-indulgence.

Usually we think of and hear about intemperance in association with alcohol. It is true that drunkenness is prohibited by Bible teaching, and we must be concerned about intemperance in this area; the author does not mean any under-emphasis on this phase of teaching. Because so much has been said about it we will go to other areas of excessiveness in this study.

One can be intemperate in eating. Gluttony, also, is prohibited by Bible teaching, but do we hear much about it? We, in affluent America, are eating ourselves to death. All social amenities call for careful planning of sufficient and proper foods. We are constantly offered food, coffee, tea, soft drinks - on every occasion when people get together, and many times hosts and hostesses are so insistent it embarrasses a guest to refuse, even when accepting it may be harmful to their health.

In our present fun-oriented world there is intemperance in fun and games! Who are the highest salaried people in our culture? *The entertainers!!* We watch football players and other athletes torture their broken and pain-racked bodies in pursuit of the sport and to please the spectators. In the art and theatrical world the show must go on. We no longer tell our children to "Be Good", when they go out, but we tell them to "Have Fun".

Much of the pressure of our time is caused by keeping up the pace with all the cultural and entertainment billings that are expected of the "in" group. Weddings are such productions many times that both the bride and groom (and the parents' bank accounts) are exhausted. For what?

There is no time to study God's will for us because of the hustle and bustle required of us in keeping our children chauffered to and tutored in all of the activities of the time. A young banker was once heard to say that he was going to start an organization to unorganize, and start a stay-at-home club where meetings would require parents and children just to *stay at home together.*

At the other extreme of the pendulum's swing is intemperance in work. Some men are working such long hours that they rarely see their families. "All work and no play makes Jack a dull boy" may be a trite statement but it is true. Homes are being broken regularly because the man no longer has time to be the head of the house, to be a companion to his wife and a father to his children. There are at least three reasons for this: 1. pressure from the family for more and better things that require higher salaries and longer hours; 2. it may provide an escape hatch for the man who is evading his responsibilities as head of the home and discipliner of the family life; 3. or it may be caused by a subconscious drive and ambition to live up to a family image, or to cover some supposed inadequacy causing an inferiority complex. When this situation does not lead to a broken home it leaves it badly bent!

The man is not the only offender in this area. Many times the woman works because she had rather work at her job or profession than to be a homemaker. She may work to provide things for her family that they cannot afford on his salary. Intemperance in her working hours can deprive her children and her husband of a great deal more than she can ever provide for them. The writer does not have to leave her own block to see the devastating effect on the children of a mother who is seldom at home. NOTHING is a suitable substitute for a mother.

Re-creation is essential at times. Even Christ went aside for rest, privacy and prayer. *Recreation* that does not *re-create* is not suitable recreation. The family unit is suffering in America today because of intemperance in ambition and work.

Love hurts none. Love does not try to impress. Love is patient and kind. Are you hurting yourself with intemperance, with self-conceit, with sophistication?

LOVE YOURSELF!

Discussion Questions

1. *Name some ways people you know try to impress others.*
2. *Define sophistication.*
   a. *What does it really mean to you?*
   b. *Have you ever wished to be sophisticated?*
   c. *What advantage do you find for yourself in it?*
3. *What does Paul say in I Corinthians 1:18-31 about man's wisdom?*
4. *Define self-conceit.*
5. *What do Romans 12:3 and Galatians 6:3 mean to you?*
6. *What description did Paul give of the people in his day in his letter to Timothy in II Timothy 3:1-5.*
7. *What is the difference in loving self and thinking more highly of self than we should?*
8. *Name 5 things in which people are intemperate.*
   a. *Are you intemperate in any area of your life?*
9. *List individually the things you and your family members do for recreation.*
   a. *How many of these activities do you do together?*
   b. *Do these things re-create you?*
   c. *What is the alternative to re-creating yourself?*
10. *Do you love yourself? (Romans 13:10, Phillips).*

Chapter 13

LIVE FOR YOURSELF

Every man must give account of himself to God. (Romans 14:12.) In the second chapter of this book it was stated that the flesh goes back to the dust from which it came and the soul goes back to God who gave it, *but this is not the end of the matter!* This accounting is not a voluntary thing; every version and translation states it in a very positive way. NEB states it this way: "As I live, says the Lord, to me every knee shall bow and every tongue acknowledge God." So you see, each of us shall answer for himself.

As has been stated previously, fear of the opinion of peers — what others think — directs much of our action in life. One of the greatest influences is fear of criticism by those we respect and admire, and one of the greatest influences in youth is to do what the "in" crowd is doing.

The writer of Hebrews, in 13:5,6, quotes an Old Testament promise of God to His people, "I will never leave you nor forsake you." He applies this same promise to Christians by adding that we can confidently say, "The Lord is my helper, I will not be afraid; what can man do to me?" To *learn* this is to have a faith of our own, one which will enable us to *put pleasing God before pleasing others.* This same writer gives the example of this kind of faith in Noah, who built an ark in a dry land that had never seen rain. What must his peers have said of him! Yet, he built an ark and he and his family were saved by water. (I Peter 3:20.)

At the most, man can discomfit one only temporarily. The final accounting is of self to God. Paul said it to the Corinthians in these words: "For every one of us will have to stand without pretense before Christ our judge, and we will be rewarded for what we did when we lived in our bodies, whether it was good or bad." (II Corinthians 5:10.) Every day of life should be lived with the thought, not what will people say, but *what will God think?* To live for self is to direct one's life daily in such a way as to be able to account to God with confidence.

As has been said elsewhere in this study, we are the result of our choices. If I love myself I will *Choose Life.*

The book of Deuteronomy is a very touching book. Moses, the man to whom God talked face to face as a man talks to a friend, (Exodus 33:11), is preparing to leave the people he has led from the bondage of Egypt through the wilderness wanderings to the very border of the Promised Land. He knows their weaknesses and failings, so he repeats the law, points out the blessings of obedience and the curses of disobedience. We find him tying the loose ends, as it were, and pleading with the people to take advantage of who they are, and make the *right* choice. After setting all of this before them, in Deuteronomy 30:15, he asks them to see, "I have set before you this day life and good, death and evil." In v. 19 he calls heaven and earth to witness that he has set before them life and death, blessing and curse, "therefore, *Choose Life,* that you and your descendants may *live,* loving God, obeying His voice and cleaving to Him."

We, too, must choose life. We will *obey Him and live,* or *disobey Him and die.* The formula is that simple. To *live* is to renew the inner man, the spirit man, day by day, because the outward man decays. (II Corinthians 4:16.) Although this deterioration is more evident with the passing years it is not restricted to old age. A renewed man is one who is changed by a renewed mind, by knowledge of God; an informed mind controlled by captured thought. (Colossians 3:10, Romans 12:2, Ephesians 4:23.)

This puts us back where we started out in Chapter 2 of this book, i. e., realizing our dual nature, the *earth* (flesh) man who houses the *spirit* man. What choice will I make? Will the earth man dominate the spirit man, or will the spirit man dominate?

How can I be sure which will emerge as dominant? Let us read Galatians 5:13-15, RSV: "For you were called to freedom, brethren; only do not use your freedom as an opportunity for the flesh, but through love be servants of one another. For the whole law is fulfilled in one word. 'You shall love your neighbor as your self.' But if you bite and devour one another take heed that you are not consumed by one another.

But I say, walk by the Spirit and do not gratify the desires of the flesh. For the desires of the flesh are against the Spirit and the desires of the Spirit are against the flesh; for these are opposed to each other, to prevent you from doing what you would. But if you are led by the Spirit you are not under the law.

Now the works of the flesh are plain: immorality, impurity (of mind, Phillips), licentiousness (indecency, NEB), idolatry, sorcery, enmity (quarrels, NEB), selfishness, dissension, party spirit, envy, drunkenness, carousing, and the like. I warn you, as I warned you before, that those who do such things shall not inherit the kingdom of God."

"And if anyone's name is not found written in the Book of Life he was thrown into the lake of fire. This is the second death." (Revelation 20:14,15.)

"But the fruit of the Spirit is love, joy, peace, patience, kindness, goodness, faithfulness (fidelity, NEB), gentleness, self-control; against such there is no law. And those who belong to Christ Jesus have crucified the flesh with its passions and desires". (Read Revelation 21:1-22:5 for the word picture of the abode of those whose names are found in the Book of Life.)

"If we *live* by the Spirit, let us also *walk* by the Spirit." Which will you choose? Will you choose the works of the flesh and the second death, which is torment day and night for ever and ever in the lake of fire, or will you choose the fruit of the Spirit, and the eternal abode in God's presence?

Much frustration is caused by our attitude toward our necessary involvement with people. Christianity is an involved life. It is helpful to realize that in teaching others it is not necessary to convert them to *our way* of thinking. *God's word* is the criteria; teaching should be limited to what the Bible teaches, and the choice must be left to the individual. When attending to the needs of others we are limited to putting the help before them; it is not possible to solve their problems for them, that choice must be theirs.

Sometimes our attitude in the criticism of others, when they do not conform to our way of thinking, is a greater sin than the sin of the individual being criticised.

Our responsibility lies in consecrating SELF, in getting SELF right with God, in converting SELF to God's way of thinking. Jesus taught in Matthew 6:33 to SEEK first the kingdom of God and His righteousness (all thy commandments are righteousness. Psalm 119:172), and food, clothing and shelter will be yours as well. The decision is to *CHOOSE LIFE* and good by obeying God, then letting Him guide us. One must do

what he can, when he can, where he can,

in his own realm of responsibility.

Each is to "put to death what is *earthly* in you: immorality, impurity, passion, evil desire, and covetousness, which is idolatry.

PUT OFF anger, wrath, malice, slander, and foul talking.

PUT ON compassion, kindness, lowliness, meekness, and patience, forbearing one another and forgiving one another. Above all these,

PUT ON LOVE, which binds everything together in perfect harmony". (Colossians 3:8-14).

Dear Reader, turn now to I Corinthians 13:4-8, and reread Paul's discourse on love. Substitute your own name for the word love, or charity, and read carefully and prayerfully.

LOVE NEVER ENDS! Ask yourself, "Have I put on love?"

CHOOSE LIFE AND GOOD!

LOVE YOURSELF!!

Discussion Questions

1. *What is your first reaction to the above statement?*

2. *What is the fate of every person? Romans 14:12.*

3. *What choice did Moses put before Israel just before he died?*

4. *State the simple formula for life!*
Even though the formula, per se, sounds simple, is following it an easy thing?

5. *How is the inner man renewed day by day?*

6. *In Galatians 5:13-16 how are the Galatians told to live?*

7. *What is meant by biting and devouring one another?*

8. *In order to live by the Spirit what are we to do:*
a . put off (or rid ourselves)?
b . put on (or clothe ourselves)?

9. *What is the mortar binder that holds chrisitans together in harmony?*

10. *When you read I Corinthians 13:4-8 with your name substituted for the word love, do you feel that you truly LOVE YOURSELF?*